GW01220581

Success Starts in Your Mind:

A Manual on How to Think Your Way to Success

Miranda Burnette

Copyright ©2014 Miranda Burnette

All rights reserved. No portion of this book may be reproduced in any form without written permission from the author/publisher.

Published by
Miranda Burnette Ministries

Cover Design by Jackie Moore

Printed in the United States.

ISBN: 978-0-69235-020-1

For more information or to order books contact:

Miranda Burnette Ministries, Inc.
P. O. Box 314
Clarkdale, GA 30111

Email
miranda@mirandaburnetteministries.org

Website
www.mirandaburnetteministries.org

Dedication

I dedicate this book to my husband, Morris, my two sons, Shaun and Davin, and my daughter-in-law, Maidei. They are my support team. They have encouraged me tremendously and have been very patient with me as I wrote this book. As each of them strive to fulfill their God-given potential, I want them to remember that *Success Starts in Your Mind*. I know that each of them will be successful in every area of their lives. I love you, Morris, Shaun, Davin and Maidei, and I encourage you to *Think Your Way to Success!*

Table of Contents

Introduction 1

Chapter 1: The Power of Thoughts 3

Chapter 2: What is Success? 27

Chapter 3: Think Your Way To Success 35

Chapter 4: What Do You Think about Yourself? 43

Chapter 5: You Are Who You Think You Are 55

Chapter 6: You Can if You Think You Can 59

Chapter 7: Think Big! 63

Introduction

All that a man achieves, and all he fails to achieve is the direct result of his own thoughts.
— *James Allen*

Your mind is one of the most important assets you have. It is in your mind that all things start. Thinking is one of the greatest abilities God has given to mankind.

The things that happen in your physical life first began to take shape in your thought life, because success and failure are first born in our minds before they become a reality in our lives. Ideas and dreams are also birthed in the mind.

Poverty, low self-esteem, and other negative attitudes start as seeds in the mind before we begin to act on them and live them. Prosperity, confidence, and positive attitudes also started as seeds in the mind before we began to act on and live them.

Your mind is the home of great ideas, dreams, visions, aspirations, and achievements—where all battles are lost or won.

All the information we feed into our minds affects our way of thinking. Everything starts with thoughts! Because of this, we have to choose our thoughts carefully. We shouldn't consciously think just anything that falls into our subconscious minds! A thought may pass across our mind, but we can choose whether or not to dwell on it and eventually act on it. If the thought is negative, it can lead you on the path to failure instead of on the path to success.

Your mind is the most powerful tool you can use to change the course of your life.

Chapter 1

The Power of Thoughts

Beware when the great God lets loose a thinker on this planet.
— Ralph Waldo Emerson

Let's take a moment to consider our "thought life."

The word *consider*, according to *Webster's Dictionary*, means to think about seriously, look at thoughtfully, think carefully. In other words, we need to think about what we think about, because thoughts are powerful!

- Our thoughts can help us or hurt us.
- Our thoughts can cause us to be a success or a failure.
- Our thoughts can produce victory in our lives or defeat.
- Out thoughts can help us to be in prosperity or in poverty.
- Our thoughts can cause us to be happy or sad.
- Our thoughts can help us become a leader or a follower.

The root of our problems very often starts in our "thought life." What you have put into your mind has made you what you are today. Your mind has also brought you to where you are right now.

Your thoughts affect your circumstances depending on how you respond to them, and how we respond to our circumstances depends on how we perceive and think about them.

> *The circumstances that surround a man's life are not important. How that man responds to those circumstances is important. His response is the ultimate*
> *determining factor between success and failure.*
> —Booker T. Washington

The way you use your mind and the way you choose to think determine everything you accomplish and everything you become. When you change your thought life, you change every part of your life. When considering our thought life, these are a few questions we can ask ourselves:

- Do I dwell on negative or positive thoughts most of the time?

- Does love **permeate** my thoughts or does judgment, anger or criticism have their way in my mind?

    Permeate: To flow or spread throughout; to penetrate and pass through a substance without rupture or displacement of its parts; applied particularly to fluids that pass through substances of loose textures, as: *Water permeates sand. Light permeates glass.*

When something unpleasant happens, do your thoughts start with fear or with faith? We know that the Bible tells us that the just shall live by faith, not fear.

> *Hebrews 10:38 – But the **just** shall live by faith [My righteous servant shall live by his conviction respecting man's relationship to God and divine things, and holy fervor born of faith and **conjoined** with it]; and if he draws back and shrinks in fear, My soul has no delight or pleasure in him.*
>
> **Just**: In a moral sense, upright; in an evangelical sense, righteous.
>
> **Conjoined**: To join or become joined together; united. If you are saved, you are the *just*.

If your mind is filled with doubt, fear and unbelief, if fear permeates your thoughts, you are not having faith in God. You should not fear, because God is there for you. If God is for us, who can be against us?

> *Romans 8:31 – What then shall we say to [all] this? If God is for us, who [can be] against us? [Who can be our foe, if God is on our side?]*

Our actions are a direct result of our thoughts. Your life follows a path that is set by your mind. You are setting the direction of your life with your thoughts.

Wherever your mind goes, your actions will follow. Right actions follow right thinking. Wrong actions follow wrong thinking. If your mind is a mess, your life is also going to be a mess. If you straighten out your mind, you will straighten out your life. Your life is not going to get straightened out until your mind gets straightened out.

If you want change in your life, you have to change your thoughts. Many of us will have to change mindsets (ways of thinking) that may have dictated our lives for many years.

Your Mind Is the Center of Control

The devil knows that if he can control how you think, he will be able to control your entire life. Positive minds produce positive lives! Negative minds produce negative lives!

Your Mind Is a Power Station

Even though our minds are power stations, the average person uses only 10% or less of his or her mind's unlimited potential in the course of a lifetime. This means that 90% of our brain power is wasted.

For example, Albert Einstein was the genius physicist who formulated the theory of relativity. After his death, when scientists analyzed his brain, they discovered that he used approximately 10% of his thinking capacity. It took only a small amount of extra effort on the part of Einstein—a little more extra mental effort—to produce his brilliant theories. Things that no one else had ever thought about came from Einstein's mind.

Just imagine what you could accomplish with a mind controlled by good thoughts. What could you accomplish with thoughts inspired by God and His infinite supply of wisdom? God created your mind just like He did Einstein's—for accomplishment, brilliance and success.

Think about this: If you continually think negative thoughts, you will gravitate toward negative people, activities and lifestyles. Our lives follow our thoughts. We draw in what we constantly think about just like a magnet (see Chapter 4).

On the other hand, if we are always thinking positive, happy, joyful thoughts, we are going to be positive, happy, joyful people, and we will attract other positive, happy, joyful people.

Positive thinking also produces positive attitudes. Once your attitude changes, your life will change. The exact results of your own thoughts will be placed into your hands.

No matter what your present environment or situation, you will fall or rise according to your thoughts. When thoughts that are contrary to God's Word come our way, we need to take every one of those thoughts captive to make them obedient to Christ.

That means that we must choose not to think the wrong thoughts. But, when we stop thinking the wrong thoughts, we need to replace them with good thoughts. If you are thinking about something good, the wrong things have no place to get in. But if you don't think anything at all, the wrong things are going to enter right back into your empty mind.

> *2 Corinthians 10:5 (Amplified) – [In as much as we]* **refute** *arguments and* **theories** *and* **reasonings** *and every proud and lofty thing that sets itself up against the [true] knowledge of God; and we lead every thought and purpose away captive into the obedience of Christ (the Messiah, the Anointed One),*

Refute: Prove to be false or erroneous.

Theories: Assumptions or guesses based on limited knowledge or information; opinions; views; ideas; feelings; personal judgments; attitudes; positions; popular beliefs; points of view; ways of thinking.

Reasonings: Acts or operations of the mind by which new or unknown propositions (those offered for consideration, acceptance or adoption; a proposal) are deduced from previous ones that are known and evident, or that are admitted or supposed for the sake of argument; argumentation; rationalizations; discussions; arguments.

Remember: It's not good enough to just stop thinking wrong thoughts, you have to think of a right thought. If we choose to think something good, the bad thing can't get into our minds. You may be thinking, "I can't help what I think; things just come into my head." But that's not true; we can choose to think good thoughts.

We must know God's Word in order to know Truth, and we must remove any thought that does not agree with His Word. If we don't, we will think wrong thoughts that will eventually ruin our lives and our relationships.

Your mind is like a garden. You have to keep the garden of your mind pure, just like a gardener keeps his soil free from weeds and grows just the right flowers or fruits. We have to continually cultivate and weed out all the wrong, useless, impure thoughts.

Just like a plant springs from a seed, our thoughts spring from planted seeds of thought. You have to plant the right seeds that will bring forth the right kind of fruit.

If we don't stop wild ideas and unchecked thoughts from springing up like weeds, they will begin to shape our character and, eventually, our destiny.

We don't have to use any effort to think wrong thoughts, but sometimes we have to use superb effort to think good thoughts. As we begin to make changes, we will have to fight a battle. God has given us the power to decide, to choose right thinking over wrong thinking.

Once we make the choice of right thinking, we must continue to choose right thoughts. The more we fill our lives with reading the Bible, praise, prayer, and fellowship with other believers, the easier it is for us to continue choosing right thoughts. But to think in the right way takes practice.

> 2 Corinthians 10:3-4 (KJV)
> 3. For though we walk [live] in the flesh, we do not war after [according to] the flesh,
>
> 4. For the weapons of our warfare are not carnal [physical weapons of flesh and blood], but mighty through God to the pulling down of strongholds.
>
> 5. [Cast] down imaginations, and every high thing that exalteth itself against the knowledge of God, and bringing into captivity every thought to the obedience of Christ.

These verses tell us that:
- We are in a war!
- We are in a spiritual war!
- We have spiritual weapons!
- The battleground is the mind!
- The enemy is Satan!

We also see in these verses that there are three levels of thinking:

1. Thoughts
2. Imaginations
3. Strongholds

Each of these represents a level of mental activity. Two of them are associated with behavior.

The Selection of Thoughts Is the First Level of Thinking!

Thoughts: The act or operation of the mind; meditation; serious consideration; silent contemplation; inward reasoning; a product of thinking; the act or process of thinking; reasoning; heavy thinking; working of the mind; mental labor; reflection.

You are going to be bombarded by hundreds of opportunities a day to take certain thoughts and to reject others.

> *Matthews 6:25 (KJV) – Therefore I say unto you, take no thought for your life, what you shall eat, or what you shall drink; nor yet for your body, what you shall put on. Is not the life more than meat, and the body more than raiment?*
>
> *Matthew 6:31(KJV) – Therefore take no thought, saying, "What shall we eat? or What shall we drink? or Wherewithal shall we be clothed?"*

Jesus said, "Take no thought." You have a choice. There are thoughts you should take and thoughts you shouldn't take. As stated before, you don't have to take every thought that comes to your mind. Jesus is telling us here some of the thoughts we shouldn't take:

- What we should eat
- What we should drink
- What we should wear

How do you *take* a thought? You begin taking a thought when you put words to it! When you begin voicing or putting words to something that previously was a random thought, it's the same as grabbing it. When you grab a thought (words you speak to somebody else or self-talk), you make it yours. You have latched on to it.

For example: The thought might come to you while you are on your job, "I can't do this job; I am not capable; I don't have the ability or what it takes; I just can't do this." You have just grabbed that thought. If you then say the same thoughts to another or even just out loud, you have made it your own.

You should instead have attacked that thought with the Word of God and said, "I can do all things through Christ Who strengthens me."

> *Philippians 4:3 (KJV) – I can do all things through Christ, [Who] strengthens me.*

Philippians 4:3 (Amplified) – I have strength for all things in Christ Who empowers me. [I am ready for anything and equal to anything through Him Who infuses inner strength into me; I am self-sufficient in Christ's sufficiency.]

The point is, you have a choice about the thoughts you take. You can bring them into obedience to Christ. That means that you do not put words to the thoughts that don't correspond to the standard of God's Word, and you don't take them. You can also take thoughts in line with the standards of God's Word by putting words to them.

The Second Level of Thinking Is Imagination!

Imagination: The power or faculty of the mind by which it conceives and forms ideas of things communicated to it by the organs of sense; the power of the mind to form mental images or a concept of something that is unreal or not present; creative thought; visualization; mental picture; to form a mental picture.

Imagination is the process of mental imagery. It is mentally imaging your circumstances or using the thoughts you have to build an image of your life as it relates to that particular thought pattern.

Your imagination plays a role in getting from the problem to the answer. When you imagine something, you see it in your "mind's eye."

> *Ephesians 1:18 (KJV) – The eyes of your understanding [are] being enlightened that ye may know what is the hope of His calling, and the riches of the glory of His inheritance in the saints.*
>
> *Ephesians 1:18 (Amplified) – By having the eyes of your heart flooded with light, you can know and understand the hope to which He has called you, and how rich is His glorious inheritance in the saints [His set-apart ones].*

Your mind is the eyes of your heart. Your mind is what sees what is in your spirit.

The imagination is a God-created part of every one of us, and one of the most powerful instruments we possess for getting results. The imagination comes with the supernatural ability to achieve the imagined object.

Some people use their imaginations for wrong things or in the wrong way. We all know that your imagination can get you in trouble. Unholy imaginations and fantasy have led many people into dangerous situations. If we can uncover God's creative purpose for the imagination and use it the way He intended, we will begin to get amazing, righteous results.

Using your imagination God's way can get you healed, delivered and blessed. Have you ever walked by a department store window, looked at a dress or suit and said, "Wow! I can just see myself wearing that outfit"?

Have you ever passed a new car and said to yourself, "I can see myself driving a car like that"? The fact is, you really did see yourself driving that car. How? In your mind's eye. Through the faculty of your imagination, you were able to see a reality that did not presently exist. The imagination level is where behavior begins.

Imagination is the capacity of the human mind to visualize life within the vicinity (surroundings) of the thoughts we have embraced. God created the human mind to produce mental imagery. It can be a good thing or it can be a bad thing depending on how we use it.

God talks about this in terms of vision, which is using your imagination to visualize the goal God has given you for your life, the plan He has laid out for your life.

> *Habakkuk 2:2 (KJV) – And the Lord answered me, and said, "Write the vision, and make it plain upon tables, that he may run that readeth it."*

> *Habakkuk 2:2 (Amplified) – And the Lord answered me and said, "Write the vision and engrave it so plainly upon tablets that everyone who passes may [be able to] read [it easily and quickly] as he hastens by."*

> *Habakkuk 2:2 (The Living Bible) – And the Lord said to me, "Write my answer on a billboard, large and clear, so that anyone can read it at a glance and rush to tell the others."*

This verse says that your imagination will produce positive behavior if you write the vision and make it plain. You can run (your behavior follows the process of mental imagery), or you can begin to live your life, behaviorally speaking, with that vision.

When the prophet Habakkuk said, "Write the vision, and make it plain upon tables [tablets]," he was talking about the capacity of the human mind to envision the future.

That is important because, if our imagination has produced an accurate vision of the future, it will also produce a driving force for that vision or set the vision in motion.

The prophet must write the vision so that he or she might imprint it on their own mind, and make it more clear to themselves first, so it might be noticed by those in distant places and transmitted to those in the future.

What is handed down by tradition is easily mistaken and liable to corruption, but what is written is preserved and is safe and pure.

One of the first scriptural references to the imagination occurs in Genesis 11: 4-8.

> *Genesis 11:1-8 (Amplified)*
> *1 And the whole earth was of one language and of one accent and mode of expression.*

2 And as they journeyed eastward, they found a plain [valley] in the land of Shinar, and they settled and dwelt there.

3 And they said one to another, Come, let us make bricks and burn them thoroughly. So they had brick for stone. and slime (bitumen) for mortar.

4 And they said, Come, let us build a city and a tower whose top reaches into the sky, and let us make a name for ourselves, lest we be scattered over the whole earth.

5 And the Lord came down to see the city and the tower which the sons of men had built.

6 And the Lord said, Behold, they are one people and they have all one language; and this is only the beginning of what they will do, and now nothing they have imagined they can do will be impossible for them.

7 Come, let Us go down and there confound (mix up, confuse) their language, that they may not understand one another's speech.

8 So the Lord scattered them abroad from that place upon the face of the whole earth, and they gave up building the city.

When God is talking about the tower of Babel, He says, "Nothing they have imagined to do will be restrained from them." God said they could accomplish anything they could imagine; nothing could hold them back.

Why did God say this? Because that is the way God created the mind. Their potential was so great because of the blueprint (carefully designed plan) in their imaginations. The nearly unlimited power of imagination got God's immediate attention. Because of this, He said, "I have to put a stop to this."

God came down and confused their language in order to destroy their unity, because imagination is such a powerful, creative tool. If you can learn to use your imagination in God's way, it will become a powerful weapon that cannot be defeated!

Behavior is connected with the imagination. It is when we begin to visualize our life within the context of our thoughts and words that behavior is produced.

The Third Level of Thinking Is Strongholds!

Strongholds: An area in which we are held in bondage (prison) due to a certain way of thinking. Strongholds are lies that are believed. A person who believes a lie is deceived. When an individual believes that wrong is right, he or she has fallen into deception.

How does a stronghold develop? It begins with the selection of thoughts. What thoughts are you going to grab with the words of your mouth? Once you have made a thought yours, and put a few other thoughts with it, and dwelled on it for a while, it becomes part of your imagination. You begin to visualize your life in association with that pattern of thoughts that you have made your own. And it will produce corresponding behavior.

If the behavior produced is in line with the Word of God, you need to develop it because it will benefit you. If the behavior is contrary to the Word of God, that repeated behavior will produce a bad habit that Satan can very quickly exploit and make a stronghold. He will carry that bad habit to a place that psychologists call "obsessive compulsive behavior."

Obsessive compulsive behavior feels like something you just can't seem to help, and you are confronted with many opportunities to indulge in it because the enemy of your soul (the devil) will see to it that you are confronted with those opportunities. The behavior becomes a stronghold, something hard to break free of, a yoke. And now you are in an area that requires more than just disciplining your thought life.

Now the anointing of God is needed to destroy that yoke so you can begin dealing with the negative or bad pattern of behavior, habit pattern or obsessive compulsive behavior that has produced a lower quality of life for you.

> *Isaiah 10:27 (Amplified) – And it shall be in that day that the burden of [the Assyrian] shall depart from your shoulders, and his **yoke** from your neck. The yoke shall be destroyed because of fatness [which prevents it from going around your neck].*

> **Yoke**: A clamp or vice that holds one down and controls movement; something that binds; something that restricts freedom; a form or symbol of bondage; an oppressive power.

You have to begin dealing with that behavior, and that dealing begins in the mind. Any kind of difficulty in the behavior arena is traceable to the mind so, therefore, can be changed.

For example, it's impossible to quit smoking without dealing with your thought life. People say that smoking, as well as many other bad habits, is a chemical addiction. Perhaps, but many people have a hard time getting rid of it. Actually the chemical addiction (the nicotine in your system) is over in three days, but some people struggle for years to get free of cigarettes because they don't deal with their mindset. They continue to think every moment how nice it would be to relax with a cigarette after dinner. And the difficulty continues month after month, not because of a chemical addiction, but because they are not dealing with the root of the problem.

You have to break your unhealthy thought patterns if your behavior pattern is going to change. Once the behavior becomes a stronghold, Satan is exploiting a weakness you have shown him that you have by the words of your mouth and the behavior of your body.

Once it gets to this point, breaking the stronghold requires more than mental discipline; it requires the ministry of the Holy Spirit, the anointing that destroys the yoke. It requires the power of God. How do we change our thoughts? By renewing our minds with God's Word!

> *Romans 12:2 — Do not be **conformed** to this world [this age, fashioned after and adapted to its external, superficial customs], but be **transformed** [changed] by the [entire] renewal of your mind [by its new ideals and its new attitude], so that you may prove [find out for yourself] what is the good and acceptable and perfect will of God, even the thing which is good and acceptable and perfect [in His sight for you].*

Conform: To give the same shape, bring into harmony with, be in agreement or conformity with; to adapt.

Transform: Form (trans) by moving from one place to another; change the composition or structure; change the outward form or appearance of; change in character or condition; convert.

You have to prepare yourself mentally—program your mind—for success! And we program our minds with the Word of God. God wants our minds to be transformed into His will (God's Word is His will), not conformed to the mold of the world. Christians should not think and act like worldly people. God's Word will take the place of uncontrollable thoughts, impure mental pictures, confused ideas, wandering thoughts and double-mindedness. To transform your mind, you need to fill it with God's Word.

Every person is divided into three parts: body, soul and spirit. We are tri-part beings. You are a spirit. You possess a soul. You live in a body.

Body: Hearing, seeing, smelling, touching, tasting.

Soul: Mind, will, emotions (what you think, want and feel).

Spirit: Heart (when the Bible refers to the heart of a person, it is referring to your spirit).

After giving, or surrendering, your life to Christ, your spirit is reborn and given new life. This is where we get the term "born again." Although the condition of your spirit changes automatically when you accept Jesus, your soul and body do not. You must make the effort to renew, or transform, your mind so your thoughts agree with the Word of God. Only then will your mind, will, emotions and actions begin to line up with the desires of your spirit.

After accepting Jesus as your Lord and Savior, it's very important that you study and apply the Word of God to your life daily. Until this transformation takes place, your mind will still think worldly thoughts, and you will continue to fall prey to the same temptations as before.

This is what leads others to believe that many Christians are hypocrites but, just because an individual fails to overcome temptation doesn't mean that he or she is not a Christian. To renew our minds with the Word of God, we can read the Word, pray the Word, listen to the Word being preached, listen to the Word being taught, read books with the Word in them, and listen to the Word on tapes or CDs. Your mind is being renewed right now by reading this book.

Don't just read God's Word, however. Also meditate on it, think on it throughout the day, and ask the Holy Spirit to reveal insight to you. When we read the Word of God, we get information. When we study or meditate on the Word of God, we get revelation.

Revelation: The act of disclosing (revealing or making known) or discovering what was before unknown; the communication of truth to man by God Himself; that which is revealed; an act of revealing; a manifestation of divine will or truth; something disclosed, especially something not previously known or revealed.

When we get revelation, we know that we know that we know, and no one, not even the devil, can take it away from us. Having a revelation means that, one day, you suddenly understand something to the point that it becomes part of you.

The knowledge isn't only in your mind. You no longer need to renew your mind to it because you don't wonder or hope it's true; you know it's true.

> *Ephesians 4:22-23 – Strip yourself of your former nature [put off and discard your old unrenewed self] which characterized your previous manner of life and becomes corrupt through lusts and desires that spring from delusions.*

And be constantly renewed in the spirit of your mind (have a fresh mental and spiritual attitude.) Don't let negative thinking hold you back.

> *Romans 8:5 (Amplified) – For those who are according to the flesh and are controlled by its unholy desires set their minds on and pursue those things which gratify the flesh, but those who are according to the Spirit and are controlled by the desires of the Spirit set their minds on and seek those things which gratify the [Holy] Spirit.*
>
> *Romans 8:5 (KJV) – For they that are after the flesh do mind the things of the flesh, but they that are after the Spirit [**mind**] the things of the Spirit.*
>
> **Mind**: To attend to, fix the thoughts on, regard with attention.

In other words, if we think fleshly thoughts, wrong thoughts, or negative thoughts, we can't walk in the Spirit. Renewed God-like thinking is a vital necessity to a successful Christian life. Your life may be in a state of chaos because of years of wrong thinking.

If your life is in chaos, you need to know that it won't get straightened out until your mind does. Remember, our weapons are the Word of God, praise and prayer.

> *Life consists of what a man is thinking about all day.*
> *—Ralph Waldo Emerson*

If we walk in the flesh, it is because we have our minds on fleshly things. If we walk in the Spirit, it is because we have our minds on Spiritual things.

> *Colossians 3:2 – And set your minds and keep them set on what is above [the higher things], not on the things that are on the earth.*

The mind is the leader of all actions! Example: If I were to think for a long time of something really bad someone did to me, how that person gossiped about me, said hurtful things to me, lied to me and about me, it would be impossible for me to treat that person as though nothing had happened.

> *The actions of men are the best interpreters of their thoughts.* —*John Locke*

Miranda Burnette

Chapter 2

What is Success?

Success is not measured by what a man accomplishes, but by the opposition he has encountered, and the courage with which he has maintained the struggle against overwhelming odds.
—*Charles Lindbergh*

If you ask the question, "What is success," you would most likely get all kinds of answers, because people measure success in different ways. Some people may say that success is measured by:

- How much money a person makes
- A professional title
- Where a person lives
- How expensive a car a person drives

All of these things are great—God wants us to have all of these. The following are definitions of *success*:

Dictionary.com: The achievement of something desired, planned or attempted.

Webster's New World College Dictionary 4th edition: A favorable or satisfactory outcome or result; something having such an outcome; the gaining of wealth, fame, rank, etc., as *a successful person;* coming about, taking place, or turning out to be as was hoped for, as *a successful mission;* having achieved success, specifically having gained wealth, fame, etc.

Roget's International Thesaurus 3rd edition: Accomplishment; victory; prosperity; fortunate outcome; achieving one's purpose; prosperous; fortunate; triumphant; victorious; winning; conquering; overcoming; triumphal.

The bottom line is that success is achieving God's plan for your life. God created each of us for a definite purpose. God does not make failures. Failure is not an option. God never fails!

Success is becoming the person God created you to be, not what someone else wants or expects you to be. True success is discovering and reaching your maximum potential. It is fulfilling God's purpose and perfect plan for your life.

How do we find and follow God's perfect plan for our lives? First we must realize and accept that God is our designer. And, when He designed us, He gave us a success manual: the Bible. If we want to know how to be successful, we can go to the success manual.

In the book of Jeremiah in this manual, God tells us about the good plan He has for us:

> *Jeremiah 29:11 — "For I know the thoughts and plans that I have for you," says the Lord, "thoughts and plans for welfare and peace and not for evil, to give you hope in your final outcome."*

According to that verse, God has a plan for each of us, a plan that should give us great hope for our future. This plan will lead us to our destiny. Until you find God's plan of success for your life, you will never be fulfilled, because that is the reason you were created. God has a perfect plan for our lives—a plan of success and not failure! It is a good plan, a great plan, an uncommon plan, a perfect plan!

God's plan will change you into a better person. It will never fail, because God never fails. He can't fail because He is God. So you don't have to worry about that. Still, you have to cooperate with God as He prepares you for the plan he has for your life.

God's plan for your life will help you to obtain true success. God's plan for your life is a divine plan—His divine directions for your life. Become the person God created you to be. Believe that you can be a success in every area of your life. And it all starts with the manual of God's Word.

The Word of God will do many things for you. As stated before, it will renew your mind.

> *Ephesians 4:22-23 (Amplified)*
> *22 Strip yourselves of your former nature [put off and discard your old unrenewed self] which characterized*

> your previous manner of life and becomes corrupt through lusts and desires that spring from delusion.
> 23 And be constantly renewed in the spirit of your mind [having a fresh mental and spiritual attitude].

The Word of God will help your emotions to be stable.

> Psalms 91:1 – He who dwells in the secret place of the Most High shall remain stable and fixed under the shadow of the Almighty [Whose power no foe can withstand].

The Word of God has the power to change you.

> 2 Corinthians 3:18 – And all of us with unveiled faces, [because we] continued to behold [in the Word of God] as in a mirror, the glory of the Lord, are constantly being transformed into His very own image in ever-increasing splendor and from one degree of glory to another; [for this comes] from the Lord [Who is] the Spirit.

The Word of God heals and delivers you from pitfalls and disaster.

> Psalms 107:20 – He sends forth His Word and heals them and rescues them from the pit and destruction.

The Word of God will lead and guide you.

> *Psalms 119:105 – Thy Word is a lamp to my feet and a light to my path.*

The Word of God keeps you from sin.

> *Psalms 119:11 – Thy Word have I hidden in my heart that I might not sin.*

Knowing the Word of God will help you be prosperous, deal wisely and be successful.

> *Joshua 1:8 (Amplified) – This Book of the law shall not depart out of your mouth, but you shall meditate on it day and night, that you may observe and do according to all that is written in it. For then you shall make your way prosperous, and then you shall deal wisely and have good success.*

> *Joshua 1:8 (KJV) – This Book of the law shall not depart out of thy mouth; but thou shalt meditate therein day and night that thou mayest observe to do according to all that is written therein; for then thou shalt make thy way prosperous, and then thou salt have good success.*

> *Joshua 1:8 (NIV) – Do not let this Book of the law depart from your mouth; meditate on it day and night so that you may be careful to do everything written in it. Then you will be prosperous and successful.*

Let's break this scripture down so we can understand it fully:

This Book of the law. The law is the Truth, information, and the quality of being in agreement with reality or fact.

Shall not depart out of thy mouth. "Mouth" means to speak the Truth as it is written in the Bible.

But thou shall meditate. Meditate is thinking seriously about it, studying, pondering and reflecting on it.

Day and night. Day and night in this verse means all the time, continuously.

That thou mayest observe to do according to all that is written therein. This phrase means to be obedient and act on it, to follow the direction it gives, and to abide by its laws.

For then thou shalt make thy way prosperous. This means that all your needs will be supplied, you will have plenty, and abundance will be your reward.

And then thou shalt have good success. You will be the person God created you to be, you will reach your maximum potential, you will be successful in every area of your life, and you will be fulfilled.

The Word of God strengthens you in difficulties and afflictions.

> *Proverbs 18:14 – The strong spirit of a man sustains him in bodily pain or trouble, but a weak and broken spirit, who can raise up or bear?*

The Word of God gives you hope.

> *Psalm 130:5 – I wait for the Lord, I expectantly wait, and in His word do I hope.*

The Word of God has the power to save your soul.

> *James 1:21 – So get rid of all uncleanness and the rampant outgrowth of wickedness, and in a humble [gentle, modest] spirit receive and welcome the Word which, implanted and rooted [in your hearts] contains the power to save your souls.*

Miranda Burnette

Chapter 3

Think Your Way To Success

Thought is the original source of all wealth, all success, all material gain, all great discoveries and inventions, and all achievement.
—Claude M. Bristol

Building our lives on the solid foundation of God's Word promises to bring great success. Foundations are very important! A foundation, according to *Webster's Dictionary*, is a basis on which a thing stands, is founded or is supported.

Everything that is built needs a foundation if it's going to last, stand or be successful. Houses need foundations. Office buildings need foundations. And yes, success needs to be built on a solid foundation.

If I tried to build a house without a foundation, every board I put in place would fall down. I might prop some of the boards up for a while against something else, but a little shaking or blowing wind will tumble it.

> *Matthew 7:24-27 – "So everyone who hears these words of Mine and acts upon them [obeying them] will be like a sensible [prudent, practical, wise] man who built his house upon the rock."*
>
> *And the rain fell and the floods came and the winds blew and beat against that house; yet it did not fall, because it had been founded on the rock.*
>
> *"And everyone who hears these words of Mine and does not do them will be like a stupid [foolish] man who built his house upon the sand."*
>
> *And the rain fell and the floods came and the winds blew and beat against that house, and it fell—and great and complete was the fall of it.*

Sometimes we see successful people who did not build their success on the solid foundation of God's Word. Then when the storms came (and they will come) and the winds blew (trials), their success came tumbling down.

On the other hand, we've seen people who built their success on the solid foundation of the Word of God. Then, when the storms came and the winds blew, they remained successful.

Sometimes people don't want to take time to build a solid foundation because it takes so much time. But, if you build your business on the foundation or principles of God's Word, it will be successful! Isn't that worth a little time?

Your success begins with the Word of God in your mind. You achieve this by meditating on the Word of God and allowing It to renew your mind to His ways of doing things. Then you will not fail! The power to do the Word comes from the practice of meditating on it! This is the key to success in every area of our lives. The Word of God has inherent power in it.

Meditating on the Word means taking God's Word, pondering it, dwelling on it, turning it over and over in your mind. What does meditating on the Word day and night empower you to do? Meditating on the Word of God helps you to do the Word and to receive revelation knowledge.

As you meditate on the Word of God, power is released to help you to do the Word. You will not do the Word of God if it is not a revelation to you, or if it is not real to you. You have to be able to comprehend what the Word really means before you can do it.

Success is a process. It is a part of our daily routine. It is in the basics of life. We need to meditate and practice God's Word until it becomes a part of us. When the Word gets inside us, the Word comes out when the pressures of this world start to squeeze us. Meditating on the Word of God is the key to success in every area of our lives.

> *Psalm 1:1-3*
> *1 Happy, blessed, fortunate, prosperous and enviable is the man who walks and lives not in the counsel of the ungodly [following their advice, their plans and purposes], nor stands [submissive and inactive] in the*

path where sinners walk, nor sits down [to relax and rest] where the scornful [and mockers] gather.

2 But his delight and desire are in the law of the Lord, and on His law [the precepts, instructions, teachings of God], he habitually meditates [ponders and studies] by day and by night.

3 And he shall be like a tree firmly planted [and tended] by the streams of water, ready to bring forth its fruit in its season; its leaf also shall not fade or wither; and everything he does shall prosper [and come to maturity].

These verses declare that if we meditate on the Word of God, our lives will be:

- Blessed
- Happy
- Prosperous
- Enviable
- Fruitful

And the enemy's lies will be erased and replaced with the unchanging and life-giving Truth of God's Word.

Success usually comes to people who regularly do things that unsuccessful people don't do. In addition, successful people think differently from unsuccessful people:

- Successful people think positively!
- Unsuccessful people think negatively.
- Successful people think big!
- Unsuccessful people think small.
- Successful people think out of the box!
- Unsuccessful people think inside the box.
- Successful people think long-range!
- Unsuccessful people think short-range.

You Can Think Your Way to the Top!

Those who go to the top think like successful people! As stated above, if we meditate (think on, ponder, mutter) the Word, rolling the Word over and over in our minds, we will do or act on the Word of God. The Word of God will renew our minds, and then we will begin to do what is right. Then, as Joshua says, we will make our way prosperous and have success. If you meditate on the Word, you will begin to do the Word. Don't let this Word depart out of your mouth.

> *You are today where your thoughts have brought you.*
> *You will be tomorrow where your thoughts take you.*
>   *—James Allen*

Success Starts in the Mind as a Seed

Wealth is first created in your mind. It starts with a seed of an idea. Ideas solve problems. When you solve problems, your wealth is released. God gives us ideas to solve problems. Your wealth is in whatever problem God has called you to solve.

There is a problem somewhere in the world, and you are the solution to that problem.

Some of you may have been praying for God to bless you and give you money for a need or desire you may have. In the meantime, God may have given you an idea that you have not yet implemented. You may be still praying and asking God to bless you, but He has already given you the inspired idea to produce the wealth. The wealth has already been created in your mind. All you have to do now, with the help of God, is create it in the natural realm. If you get a good idea, you don't have to worry about the money; the idea will produce the money.

Take a look around you and notice the buildings, schools, houses, highways, machines, ships and so forth. Everything you see that is man-made was an idea in somebody's mind before it became a reality. All of these wonderful things did not just appear. The house you live in, the car you drive, the clothes you're wearing, the chair you're sitting on, and the book you are reading right now were first ideas in someone's mind. We enjoy all of them because of a dream, idea or vision that was in somebody's imagination. When that idea was implemented, it became a reality. Ideas that are in thought form are the starting point of success. Just one right thought, followed by the right action, can change your entire life.

> *Deuteronomy 8:18 (Amplified) – But you shall [earnestly] remember the Lord your God, for it is He Who gives you power to get wealth, that He may establish His covenant which He swore to your fathers, as it is this day.*

God promised to give us the ability to get wealth. He did not promise to miraculously make us wealthy.

Steps to Thinking Your Way to Success

(1) Fill your mind with positive information (the Word of God, books, CDs, DVDs).

(2) See yourself as successful (visualize it in your mind).

(3) Think success (think positively, think big).

(4) Speak success (use the creative power of words to prophecy your future).

(5) Associate with winners (successful people).

Miranda Burnette

Chapter 4

What Do You Think about Yourself?

They can conquer who believe they can.
—*John Dryden*

You can't rise above what you think about yourself!

How you think about yourself has everything to do with what God can do through you. If we think discouraging thoughts, we will get discouraged. If we think condemning thoughts, we will come under condemnation. If we think we are a failure, we are going to keep on failing.

If you are afraid of stepping out because you are afraid of failing, you will always be a failure, because you will never even try to be a success.

If you think you will always be poor, you will be poor. If you are afraid you can't hear from God, you will never believe that God is speaking to you. If you think people don't like you, they never will like you. What you think about yourself, your self-image, your mental picture of yourself is what you will become. As I said before, our actions are a direct result of our thoughts. We must think differently if we want to live differently.

So it boils down to this: People see us the way we see ourselves. How are you seeing yourself?

> *Numbers 13:33 – There we (the scouts) saw the Nephilim [giants], the sons of Anak, who come from the giants; and we were in our own sight as grasshoppers, and so we were in their sight.*

The scouts (spies) could not get beyond their image of themselves. It was God's will for His people to conquer the giants and possess the Promised Land, but they were a complete failure because of their own self-image.

It wasn't really the giants that defeated these people, it was their poor self-image. It was their wrong attitude toward themselves. They saw others as giants and themselves as grasshoppers. The enemy saw them the same way they saw themselves.

From a more spiritual standpoint: When we think negative thoughts about ourselves, see ourselves distorted, have a negative self-image, have a bad mental picture, or have the wrong self perception, we open up the door to the devil to cause other people to see us that way and to treat us wrongly or badly as a result of how they see us.

Positive thoughts open the door for God to work in our lives.

Thoughts Determine Your Self-Image

Your self-image is the picture you carry of yourself in your mind. Each time you look at the picture (good or bad), that image becomes more deeply ingrained in your mind.

Our God-ordained destiny is limited by what we believe about ourselves. We can never reach God's full will unless we believe we can!

A person with a poor self-image may not step out even when God tries to promote him or her, because they are afraid of everything—people, failure, judgment.

Thoughts determine the outcome of our lives! You will remain where you are if all you see is what you have. Constant determination is required to avoid becoming like the world (the present condition of human affairs). It is very easy to be like the world.

The Fear of Success

We all know that many people are afraid of failure. Even you may have been afraid of failure once or twice in your lifetime. No one wants to fail; everyone wants to be a success.

But did you know that there are people who are actually afraid of success? They fear SUCCESS!

There are a number of reasons that people fear success. Some are concerned about what others will think of them, how others will treat them, or what others will expect of them when they become successful. They are also concerned about being rejected by others who are not at their current level of success.

> *I can't give you the formula for success, but I can give you the formula for failure: Try to please everybody.*
> *—Henry Bayard Swope*

Another reason for fear of success is a negative self-image. A person with a negative self-image may feel as if he or she is not worthy of success, or do not deserve to be successful, have the higher position, or earn more money than their peers. Their self-image, the way they see themselves, is not accurate.

He or she may doubt whether they have the ability necessary to handle the responsibilities or do what is expected. They may feel inadequate. They may not feel capable enough to handle a new position or the success that comes with it. They may have a lack of self-approval. He or she doesn't see himself as being successful in their mind's eye. Therefore, they may feel like they don't deserve the success. Because of this, they may sabotage (undermine, damage, hurt, harm, lose) their own success *unconsciously* because they aren't equipped to handle it.

Some people sabotage their success by self-destructive behaviors. Their achievement exceeds the level of their expectation. That is another example of how success starts in the mind. You have to be mentally and emotionally equipped to handle success. You need to grow mentally and emotionally as you achieve success in your life. (Source: *Living Your Dreams*, Brown L., 1992, New York, NY: Harper Collins Publications.) Success is also feared because of the weight that is attached to it, the weight we place on what it means to be successful. Some people think that success means that you are wiser or smarter than others. Some also believe that, because you are successful, you are therefore superior or better than other people. When people believe that success validates them as being good and whole and right and true, it makes success scary to them.

Success is fearful to some people because it never does any of those things. It never makes a person wiser or smarter. Neither does success validate a person or make a person perfect. If you believe that it will do these things for you, success becomes frightening. (Source: www.lazaris.com/publibrary/pubfear.cfm.)

What the Fear of Success really Means

Use this list to try to determine if the fear of success is holding you back from becoming successful.

- The fear of success is the belief that you are undeserving of all the good things and the recognition that comes your way as a result of your successes.

- The fear of success is the fear of accomplishment and being recognized and honored for your accomplishments.

- The fear of success is the lack of belief in your own ability to maintain the progress, and the accomplishments, you have achieved in your life.
- The fear of success is the belief that no matter how much you are able to accomplish, it will never be enough for you to remain successful.

- The fear of success is the belief that success is an end in itself, and yet that end is not enough to keep you interested and committed.

- The fear of success is the belief that there are others out there who are better than you, who will disgrace or replace you if you don't maintain your level of performance.

- The fear of success is the fear that once you have achieved the goals you have worked so hard for, your motivation to continue will go away.

- The fear of success is the belief that you will not do as well as others in you field, or that you are not as good as they are.

Negative Consequences of the Fear of Success

- You may lose your desire or motivation to achieve, grow or succeed.

- You may lack the effort to achieve your goals.

- You may acquire self-destructive behavior—trip yourself up to make sure you don't maintain a certain level of success.

- You may sabotage (treacherous, faithless, deceitful, victimized betrayal action to defeat or hinder a cause or endeavor) your success.

- You may choose to do the opposite of what you need to do to be successful. (Source: http://www.coping.org /growth/success.htm.)

Our thoughts are Seeds!

What we sow is what we are going to reap.

> *Galatians 6:7 – Do not be deceived and **deluded** and misled; God will not allow Himself to be sneered at [scorned, disdained, or mocked by mere pretensions or professions, or by His precepts being set aside]. [He inevitably deludes himself who attempts to delude God.] For whatever a man sows, that and that only is what he will reap.*

Delude: To deceive the mind or judgment of.

Your thoughts are seeds you sowed for an attitude you will have and an action you will take. Your own thoughts can make you sad or happy. Wrong thoughts can discourage you or even depress you.

The Law of Attraction

What you think about the most is what your mind attracts to you! Have you ever thought of someone and, a short while later, that person calls or you see them at the store. You say, "I was just thinking about you."

This happens because your mind has more power than you can imagine. If you think poverty, that is what you are going to attract. If you think danger, you are going to attract danger. If you think "Nobody likes me," nobody will like you.

On the other hand, if you think of prosperity, that is what you are going to attract. You may think of starting a business, and begin to meet people who have ideas or information about that business. Poverty-minded people tend to attract poverty. Prosperity-minded people tend to attract money-making ideas and opportunities.

The people you associate with can also determine how high you can go in life. Wrong associates can shut doors of opportunities for you by keeping away the right kinds of people and by attracting the wrong kinds of people.

People are like magnets. They attract situations and people in harmony with their thought life. People of greatness attract people of greatness. Criminals also attract each other.

If you constantly think about your past, you are going to be locked into your past. In other words, your life will continue to repeat what has happened to you in the past.

When you sow positive seeds, you reap a positive harvest. You attract people with a positive outlook on life.

God has placed greatness inside you. You should be so possessed with greatness that, when you go to bed at night, greatness is what you think about.

Greatness: Power; strength or extent of intellectual faculties, as *the greatness of genius;* bigness; largeness.

When you wake up, think about your vision. Sing about it; dream about it. In other words, you and your vision become one, and you should refuse anybody who speaks against your vision. Don't linger in their presence. You have to protect your vision. God gave you your vision; it's part of who you are.

You have a mission. An apple tree has a mission to produce apples. If you are a goldmine, you are supposed to be producing gold. If you are a goldmine and you are producing apples, something is wrong. You have the wrong programming. In other words, you have been taught that you are an apple, but you are not an apple.

Who are you? Why are you here? What is your purpose?

Your mind needs to be programmed with the Word of God, reprogrammed with God's thoughts so you can see the possibilities instead of the impossibilities.

Matthew 12:34-37
34 You offspring of vipers! How can you speak good things when you are evil [wicked]? For out of the fullness [the overflow, the superabundance] of the heart, the mouth speaks.

35 The good man, from his inner good treasure, flings forth good things; and the evil man, out of his inner evil storehouse, flings forth evil things.

36 But I tell you, on the day of judgment, men will have to give account for every idle [inoperative, nonworking] word they speak.

37 For by your words you will be justified and acquitted, and by your words you will be condemned and sentenced.

What we think in our hearts (mind or inner person) will cause either good or evil to come out of our mouths. To sum it all up, what we think eventually comes out of us in some form or fashion—in actions, attitudes, moods or words. Therefore, thoughts can affect our personal relationships and our emotions.

Our emotions respond to, and allow us to feel, what we are thinking. If you go around thinking sad thoughts, you are going to feel sad. On the other hand, if you go around thinking happy thoughts, you are going to feel happy.

Thoughts can affect our health as well. They can create good or bad, happy or sad, moods. They affect our feelings because we feel exactly the way we think. Most of our problems are rooted in thinking patterns that produce the problems we experience. When we learn how to change our way of thinking and understand how our minds work, function, and are supposed to be programmed, we will not have a lot of the problems we suffer.

Our thoughts determine our behavior. If we want bad behavior to stop, we have to stop bad thinking. When we change our way of thinking, we will change our behavior. In other words, if you want to change the quality of your life, you have to change your behavior, and to change your behavior, you have to change your mind. You can't change your actions without changing your mind.

> *Ephesians 4:22-24*
> *22 Strip yourselves of your former nature [put off and discard your old unrenewed self] which characterized your previous manner of life and becomes corrupt through lusts and desires that spring from delusion.*
>
> *23 And be constantly renewed in the spirit of your mind [having a fresh mental and spiritual attitude].*
>
> *24 And put on the new nature [the regenerate self] created in God's image, [Godlike] in true righteousness and holiness.*

In other words, stop doing the wrong thing and start doing the right thing! Choose your thoughts according to where you want to go in life. It all starts with your thoughts!

You can never rise any higher than your thoughts. You will never go beyond where you think you can go. You will never have any more than what you think you can have. You will never do any more than what you think you can do. We have not because we ask not. Prayer is another spiritual weapon that is available to us when it comes to fighting the battle in our minds.

> *James 4:2 – You are jealous and covet [what others have] and your desires go unfulfilled [so] you become murderers. [To hate is to murder as far as your hearts are concerned.] You burn with envy and anger and are not able to obtain [the gratification, the contentment, and the happiness that you seek], so you fight and war. You do not have because you do not ask.*

If you believe what the Word of God says you are, that is what you will become. If you believe what the devil says you are, you will become that. The choice is yours!

Success Starts in Your Mind

Chapter 5

You Are Who You Think You Are

A man is literally what he thinks, his character being the complete sum of all his thoughts.
—James Allen

Proverbs 23:7 (KJV) – ... *as [a man] thinketh in his heart, so is he* ...

Proverbs 23:7 (another translation) – *As a man thinks in his heart, so does he become.*

The way you use your mind and the way you choose to think determine everything you become and everything you accomplish in your life. Therefore, you should feed your mind with statements that are consistent with what you want to become. You must become the person you want to be on the *inside* before you change on the *outside*.

It is not what you are, but what you think you are, that defeats you. When you think you are imperfect, incomplete and unrighteous, you are. When you think you are defeated, you are defeated.

The life you have now is a result of thoughts you have meditated on in the past. Your thoughts have a lot to do with where you are right now, and they will have a lot to do with where you are going to end up in the future.

The way you think is the kind of person you will become. Proverbs 23:7 lets us know how important it is that we think properly. Thoughts are powerful! According to Proverbs, thoughts have creative ability! Our thoughts affect what we become. The mind is the leader of all action. It is an absolute necessity that you get your thinking in line with God's Word. Your mind prepares you for action, for victory, for success.

Your actions are a direct result of your thoughts. You can't have a positive life and a negative mind. If you have a negative mind, you will have a negative life. You can't be a success if you are continually thinking failure thoughts.

If we think we are unable to do certain things, we will be rendered unable, even though God's Word says we can do anything God asks us to do because of His ability in us.

There is a direct relationship between a person's level of thinking and their level of success. You will never go higher than your level of thinking. Your thoughts are just that powerful! You can never rise above what you think of yourself.

Your thought life, or what you think, will determine what kind of job you have, what you earn, where you live, the type of friends you have, and ultimately how far you go in life.

Remember Proverbs 23:7, "As a man thinks, so is he or so will he become." When you think thoughts of failure, you are destined to fail. If you don't think you can be successful, then you never will be!

Your thinking shapes who you are! Your thought life sets the limits on what you can become, how high you can go, or what level of achievement you can obtain. Is what you think about—your thought life, your thought pattern, your mental picture of yourself, your mentality—what you want to become?

If not, you had better change your thinking, because by changing your thinking you can change your life, and you can change your thinking with the Word of God!

> *John 8:31-32*
> *31 So Jesus said to those Jews who had believed in Him, "If you abide in My word [hold fast to My teachings and live in accordance with them], you are truly My disciples.*
>
> *32 "And you will know the Truth, and the Truth will set you free."*

Normally, people don't want to face their problems because that hurts. The truth hurts, but it is the Truth that will set us free.

Success Starts in Your Mind

We can win the victory over the lies of Satan by getting the knowledge of God's Truth in us. We can renew our minds with God's Word. If you stay in God's Word, you are one of His disciples. You are being taught by Him, because Jesus is the Word.

It is the Truth that sets you free from your problems. You can't hide behind a bunch of excuses and ever get free. You have to face the things that you do and the ways that the enemy operates through you. You have to face the Truth and say, "I have the right of free choice, and nobody is making me do this. Help me Jesus, I have a problem!"

Do you see yourself as

or

Chapter 6

You Can if You Think You Can

Don't let what you can't do interfere with what you can do. —John Wooden

Philippians 4:8 – For the rest, brethren, whatever is true, whatever is worthy of reverence and is honorable and seemly, whatever is just, whatever is pure, whatever is lovely and lovable, whatever is kind and winsome [winning, charming] and gracious, if there is any virtue and excellence, if there is anything worthy of praise, think on and weigh and take account of these things [fix your mind on them].

Your life today is a result of your thinking yesterday! Your life tomorrow will be determined by what you think today! —John Maxwell

This doesn't mean that we can do anything we want to do or anything someone else does. It means that we are able to do whatever God's will is for us to do.

You can't be a success with a failure mentality. This is one of my favorite poems:

The Man Who Thinks He Can

If you think you are beaten, you are;
If you think you dare not, you don't.
If you'd like to win, but think you can't
It's almost a cinch you won't.
If you think you'll lose, you're lose,
For out in the world we find
Success begins with a fellow's will;
It's all in the state of mind.
If you think you're outclassed, you are.
You've got to think high to rise.
You've got to be sure of yourself before
You can ever win a prize.
Life's battles don't always go
To the stronger or faster man;
But sooner or later, the man who wins
Is the one who thinks he can.
—Walter D. Wintle

Remember, the mind is where the war is won or lost. That's where Satan drops his bombs. The devil is a liar, the father of lies. The Truth is not in him. He doesn't know the Truth, nor does he know anything about the Truth.

If you are a student of the Word of God, when the lies of the enemy (the devil) come into your mind, you will have some Truth to compare them to. Then you will be able to cast down those imaginations and every high and lofty thing that exhausts itself against the knowledge of the Word of God.

Know the Word, so that when the devil lies to you, you will know it's a lie. You can't know it's a lie if you don't know the Word.

> *Corinthians 10:4 – For the weapons of our warfare are not physical [weapons of flesh and blood], but they are mighty before God for the overthrow and destruction of strongholds.*

Maybe you have been losing the battle of the mind up to now, but I believe you are going to win that war now because you have some ammunition to fight with.

Be responsible for your thoughts! Take an inventory of your thought life. If you start to feel depressed, ask yourself, "What have I been thinking about?" If you start to feel sorry for yourself, ask yourself, "What have I been thinking about?" If you start to feel angry, ask yourself, "What have I been thinking about?"

We should choose our thoughts carefully. We should not just think anything that falls into our minds. We must realize that our thoughts have a lot to do with our future. You can think your way to success!

Success Starts in Your Mind

Watch your thoughts; they become words.
Watch your words; they become actions.
Watch your actions; they become habits.
Watch your habits; they become character.
Watch your character; it becomes your destiny.
  —*Frank Outlaw*

Chapter 7

Think Big!

Nothing limits achievement like small thinking.
Nothing expands possibilities like unleashed thinking.
           —William Arthur Ward

We should not have little ideas, little dreams, or little visions! Little things are important, and we should not despise the days of small beginnings, but we ought to have big dreams because we serve a big God!

> *Ephesians 3:20-21*
> *20 Now to Him Who, by [in consequence of] the [action of His] power that is at work within us, is able to [carry out His purpose and] do **superabundantly**, far over and above all that we [dare] ask or think [infinitely beyond our highest prayers, desires, thoughts, hopes or dreams].*
>
> *21 To Him be glory in the church and in Christ Jesus throughout all generations forever and ever. Amen [so be it].*

> **Abundant**: Plentiful; in great quantity; full; sufficient, as *an abundant supply*. In scripture, abounding; having in great quantity; overflowing with.

Ephesians 3:20 tells us that God is able to do exceedingly above and beyond all we can hope, ask or even think. Why shouldn't we think big? You can't dream a dream too big for God, because God is able to do abundantly, above and beyond all we can ever hope, ask or think! We can't think too big for God!

If you are not thinking, hoping or asking for big things, you are cheating yourself. You need to think big thoughts, dream big dreams and ask for big things. God wants to do more for you than you can even ask or think!

> *Mark 10:27 – Jesus glanced around at them and said, "With men [it is] impossible, but not with God; for all things are possible with God."*

All things are possible with God, but we have to stop limiting Him in our thinking. God can open doors no man can shut!

> *Revelation 3:8 – I know your [record of] works and what you are doing. See! I have set before you a door wide open which no one is able to shut; I know that you have but a little power, and yet you have kept My Word and guarded My message and have not renounced or denied My name.*

> Romans 8:31 (KJV) – If God be for me, who can be against me?

> Hebrews 13:6 (TLB) – If God is on my side, what can mere man do unto me?

With God on your side, you cannot be defeated!

> You and God make a majority in your community.
> —Dr. Bob Jones, Sr.

> Hebrews 13:5 – Let your character or moral disposition be free from love of money [including greed, avarice, lust and craving for earthly possessions] and be satisfied with your present [circumstances and what you have], for [God] Himself has said, "I will not in any way fail you nor give you up nor leave you without support. [I will] not, [I will] not, [I will] not in any degree leave you helpless nor forsake nor let [you] down [relax My hold on you]! [Assuredly not!]"

We need to think about how big and great is the God we serve. We serve the God who created the universe!

> Hebrews 11:3 – By faith we understand that the worlds [during the successive ages] were framed [fashioned, put in order, and equipped for their intended purpose] by the Word of God, so that what we see was not made out of things which are visible.

God upholds and maintains the universe by the Word of His power. We serve a God Who used words to create the heavens and the earth.

> *Ephesians 1:19 – And [so that you can know and understand] what is the immeasurable and unlimited and surpassing greatness of His Power in and for us who believe, as demonstrated in the working of His mighty strength.*

The power of God is:

- Immeasurable – You can't quantify the power of God.

- Unlimited – God's power has no limits.

- Surpassing – The greatness of God's power passes everything else. It is the power that is above and beyond ordinary power. It exceeds, goes beyond, excels.

God said, in Isaiah 43:19, "I am doing a new thing." God wants to do a new thing in your life, but He is waiting for you to think big!

> *Romans 12:2 - Do not be conformed to this world [this age], [fashioned after and adapted to its external, superficial customs], but be transformed [changed] by the [entire] renewal of your mind [by its new ideals and its new attitude], so that you may prove [for*

> *yourselves] what is the good and acceptable and perfect will of God, even the thing which is good and acceptable and perfect [in His sight for you].*

Don't be conformed to this world or poured into its mold. Think differently. Think positively. Think about something new. Think big. God has a will for each and every one of us that includes success, prosperity and big things.

The Bible lets us know that we can do everything God asks us to do with the help of Christ, Who gives us the strength and power.

We also need to use faith filled words.

> Matthew 17:19-20
> 19 Then the disciples came to Jesus and asked privately, "Why could we not drive it out?"
>
> 20 He said to them, "Because of the littleness of your faith [your lack of firm relying trust]. For truly I say to you, if you have faith [that is living] like a grain of mustard seed, you can say to this mountain, 'Move from here to yonder place,' and it will move and nothing will be impossible to you."

We should pray daring prayers. We shouldn't let a few negative circumstances and a few disadvantages stop us. That is a trick of the devil. Don't give up; help is on the way. Be opened-minded and refuse to think little thoughts that will lead to living little lives! Think big thoughts that will lead to living big lives. God wants us to live abundant lives. God wants us to have overflow! Not just enough. He doesn't want us to lack for anything.

> *Philippians 4:19 (Amplified) – And my God will liberally supply [fill to the full] your every need according to His riches in glory in Christ Jesus.*

God wants us to live the good life, to prosper and be in health as our soul prospers.

> *3 John 2 (Amplified) – Beloved, I pray that you may prosper in every way and [that your body] may keep well, even as [I know] your soul keeps well and prospers.*

We have to be open to new ideas. The word *impossible* has to come out of our vocabulary. Why can't an ordinary person do something great? Leave ordinary things behind; think about doing extraordinary things.

Extraordinary: Beyond or out of the common order or method; not in the usual customary or regular course; not ordinary; exceeding the common degree or measure; remarkably uncommon.

Think about doing something that nobody else has done. Think aggressively. We are supposed to multiply!

> *Genesis 1:28 - And God blessed them and said to them, "Be fruitful, multiply, and fill the earth, and subdue it [using all its vast resources in the service of*

God and man]; and have dominion over the fish of the sea, the birds of the air, and over every living creature that moves upon the earth."

We are not supposed to be living little bitty lives when we serve a great big God. Small thinkers believe that things can only be done their way. They also think that things can only be done one way. Small thinkers only believe in the natural, but God is saying, "I want you to think *supernaturally*."

Remember: God is a big God. He has some expanded things in place for us. God wants us to think positively. He wants us to get the word *impossible* out of our vocabulary. He wants us to think big, to expand our borders. There is nothing too hard for God. So what is stopping you? You are limiting God with your small thinking.

Example: A number of years ago, before I bought the house that the Lord blessed me with, I was thinking about renting a small apartment, but God had bigger plans for me that I may have thought were impossible. God wanted me to own my own home. At one time, my ministry was being operated within another ministry, but the Lord also wanted me to have my own ministry.

God is trying to bless us, but some of us think that what *we* are doing is better. To that, God says:

> *Isaiah 55:8 – "For my thoughts are not your thoughts, neither are your ways My ways," says the Lord.*

We have to start thinking on a higher level, like God thinks—supernaturally! We will begin to think like God when we renew our minds with the Word of God, because the Word is His thoughts.

> *John 5:38 (Amplified) – And you have not His word [His thought] living in your hearts, because you do not believe and adhere to and trust in and rely on Him Whom He has sent. [You do not keep His message living in you, because you do not believe in Jesus Christ.]*

God's Word is also His will for our lives. We need to get into God's presence and spend time with Him so we can begin to think like He thinks.

If you start spending regular quality time with God, you can't help but think like He thinks and act like He acts. You can be transformed in the presence of God. Everything you need is in the presence of God. How big we think determines the size of our accomplishment.

> *Where success is concerned, people are not measured in inches or pounds, or college degrees, or family background; they are measured by the size of their thinking.   —Professor David J. Schwartz*

It is important to be a dreamer—a big dreamer. You need to let the Holy Spirit use your imagination to paint a picture of all God has for you. Use your imagination to see your life being worked out, the way you want it to be.

> *Isaiah 54:2 – Enlarge the place of your tent, and let the curtains of your habitations be stretched out; spare not [don't hold back]; lengthen your cords and strengthen your stakes.*

God is telling us this because we are going to expand on the right and on the left with blessings. He is saying to get ready for increase. Like Bishop T. D. Jakes says, "Get Ready, Get Ready, Get Ready."

We have to be ready for what God has prepared for us. We have to do our part. We have to prepare for it. Small thinking brings small results and big thinking brings big results.

God is letting us know not to make small plans. The Lord wants us to have big visions, big dreams and big plans. God wants to do things in our lives that will surprise us. He wants to bless us with increase. He wants to bless us supernaturally, but you and I have to prepare for it, get ready for it. The first place we start preparation is in our minds. The Lord wants to do a new thing in your life. Are you ready for it?

If God wants to do something new in your life, you may have to think a little bigger than what you have been thinking in the past. As long as you can't see the vision, it is not going to happen for you. You have to see it in the Spirit. You have to see it with your mind's eye.

> *Ephesians 1: 18 – By having the eyes of your heart flooded with light, ... you can know and understand*

> *the hope to which He has called you and how rich is His glorious inheritance in the saints [His set-apart ones].*

If you don't think you can have something good, you never will. We have to conceive it on the inside before we can ever receive it on the outside. To conceive it, you must have an image on the inside of what you want on the outside.

Start seeing yourself rising to a new level. The barrier is in your mind. It is not your lack of talent. Our small thinking can keep us from the big things God has in store for us. We must make room for increase in our thinking. We have to think big. Get rid of the old wineskins.

> *Matthew 9:17 – Neither is new wine put in old wineskins; for if it is, the skins burst and are torn in pieces, and the wine is spilled and the skins are ruined. But new wine is put into fresh wineskins, and so both are preserved.*

In other words, you can't pour new ideas into old thinking or old attitudes. Long ago, wine was stored in leather wineskins. Animal skins were dried and cured, then the leather was shaped into containers to hold the wine. They often lost their elasticity as they aged. They would become hardened and set, and they were unable to expand. If someone poured new wine into an old wineskin, the container would burst and the wine would be lost.

Jesus encouraged His followers to enlarge their visions by saying to them, "You cannot put new wine into old wineskins." Jesus was saying that you can't have a large life with limited mindsets (old thinking patterns).

What Jesus told His followers is also what He is telling us. Many of us are set in our ways. How is God going to do something new in our lives when we are hanging on to our old ways of thinking?

We need to get rid of those old wineskins and that small-minded thinking and start thinking big. Think more than enough. Think abundance. Enlarge your vision. Remember: Your life is not going to change until you change your thinking. Think big!

Let's see how we can enlarge or magnify (make larger than everything else) our thinking. Whatever we meditate on is what we magnify. Whatever we focus on grows larger in our eyes. We can magnify our weaknesses or our strengths. We can magnify the problem or the solution. We can magnify the circumstances or what the Word of God says about our circumstances. We can magnify what people say about us or what God says about us. We can magnify the bad in a person or the good. What are you focusing on? What are you magnifying?

We need to see what can be, not just what is. Big thinkers don't look at things as they are, but as they could be. A big thinker always visualizes what can be done in the future.

For example: A school teacher who only thinks of Bob as he is—an ill-mannered, disrespectful and disruptive student—will not help Bob's development. But the teacher who sees Bob not as he is now, but as he can be, will get results.

It isn't what you are right now that's important; it's what God is planning for you to be. It isn't what you did in the past, but what you are planning to do in the future. Don't focus on the past, focus on the future. Start visualizing yourself not as you are, but as you can be. You are better than you think you are!

Grow big by thinking big! Success starts in your mind. Think your way to success!

About the Author

Miranda Burnette is the president and founder of Miranda Burnette Ministries, Inc. She is also a licensed evangelist. She travels and holds Success Seminars that teach people how to discover and fulfill their calling, to make their dreams a reality, to be successful in every area of their lives, and to be all that God intended for them to be. The vision of Miranda Burnette Ministries is to educate, equip and empower others to reach their full God-given potential and to be successful leaders.

Miranda is the author of *Dare to Dream and Soar Like an Eagle, The Sky's the Limit!* Miranda hosts a weekly radio program, *Keys to Successful Living.* She also makes an impact on the lives of others with her teachings on CD and DVD.

Miranda and her husband, Morris lives in Atlanta, Georgia and are the parents of two adult children, Shaun and Davin.

Printed in Great Britain
by Amazon.co.uk, Ltd.,
Marston Gate.